THINK TANK!

THE HUMAN BRAIN AND HOW IT WORKS

ANATOMY FOR KIDS
CHILDREN'S BIOLOGY BOOKS

Baby iQ
Builder Books
EDUCATIONAL BOOKS FOR KIDS

Who is the boss in your body?
Who controls your every move?
What helps you become
smart and wise?

Your brain does it all! You breathe! Your heart beats! Your eyelids blink! You think a thought! Because the brain is working. Kids, read amazing facts about the human brain and be thrilled with how it works.

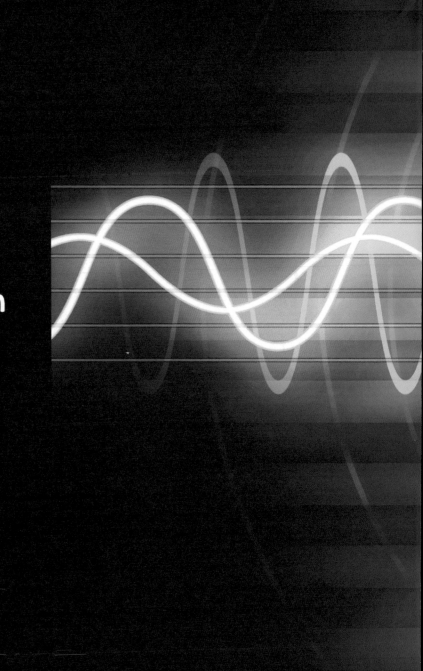

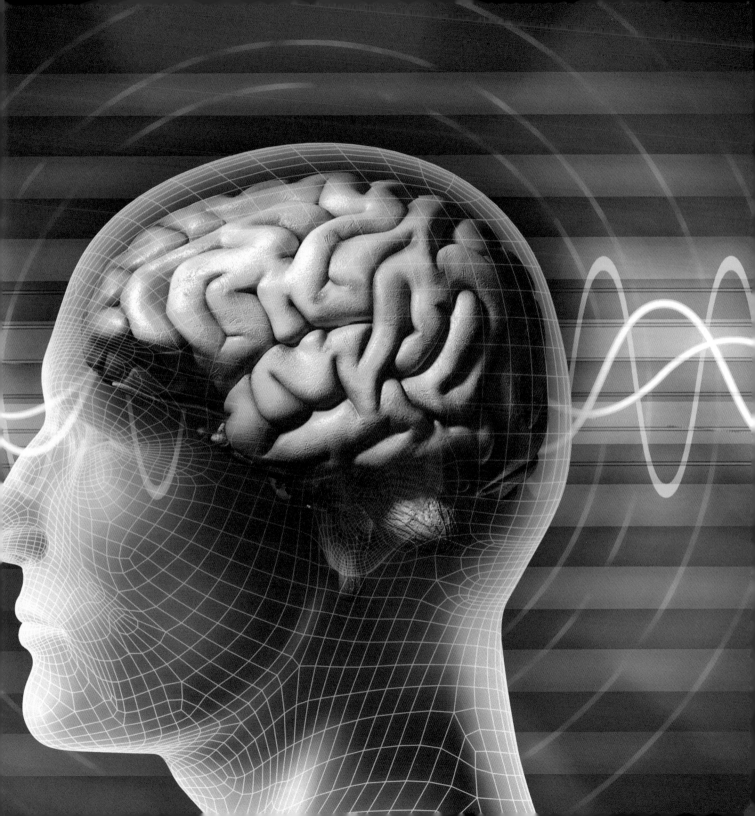

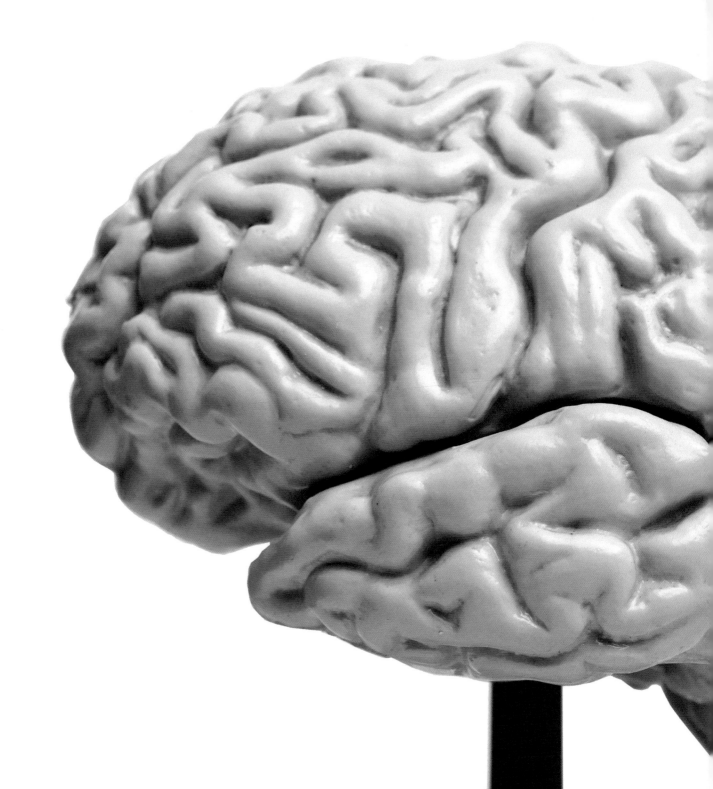

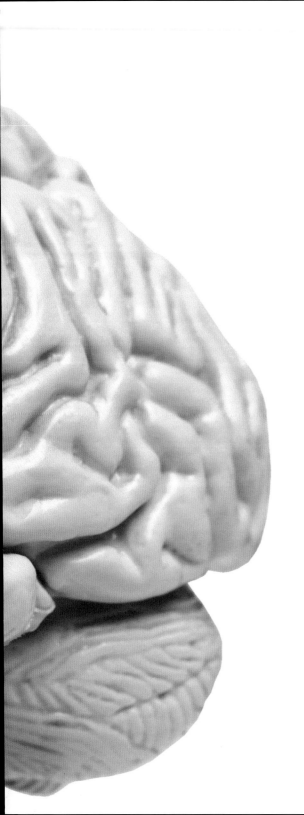

Birds have brains. Reptiles have them, too. Different mammals have brains, as well. But the human brain is fantastic. It gives us the power of speech, the ability to solve problems, and much more.

The human brain is often described as faster than the fastest computer. Yes, it is like a powerful computer. It stores our memory and tells us how we react and think. The brain dictates to most of our muscles when to contract and relax.

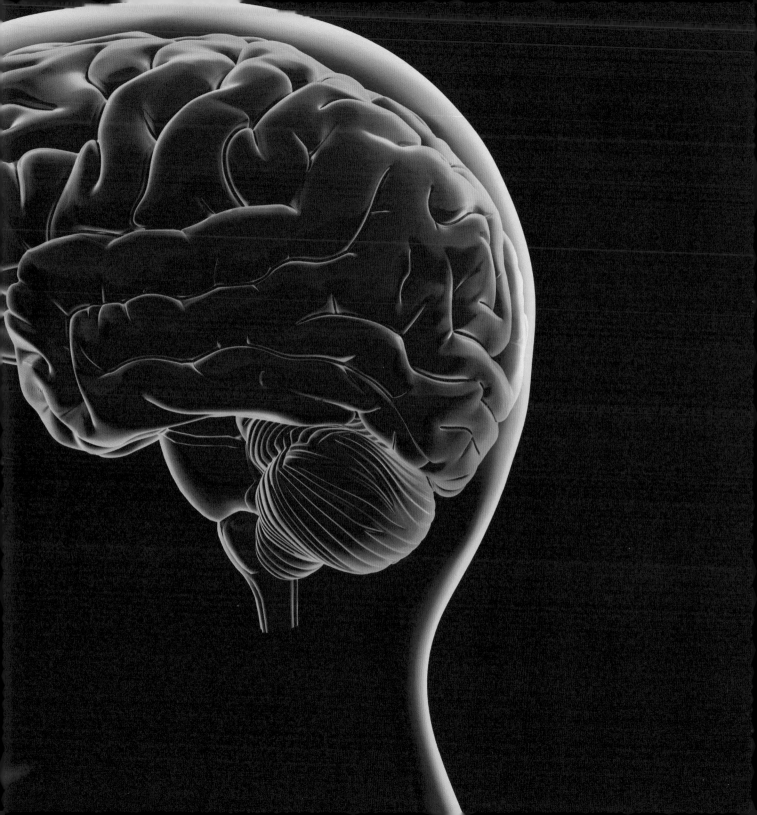

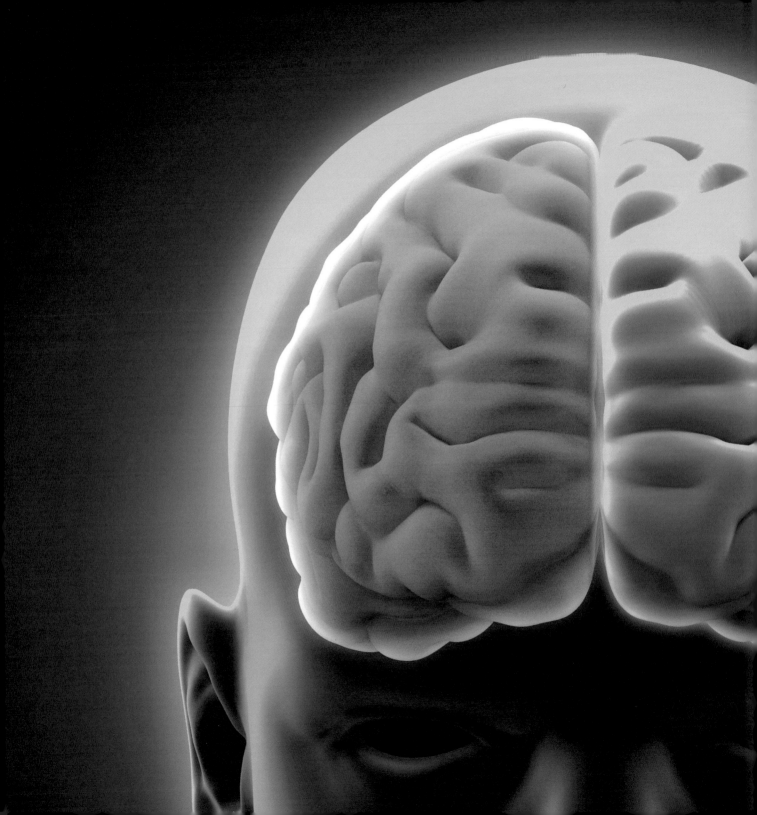

Our brain lets us know when to cry and to laugh, when to shout and when to stay calm. We feel different emotions because of our brain.

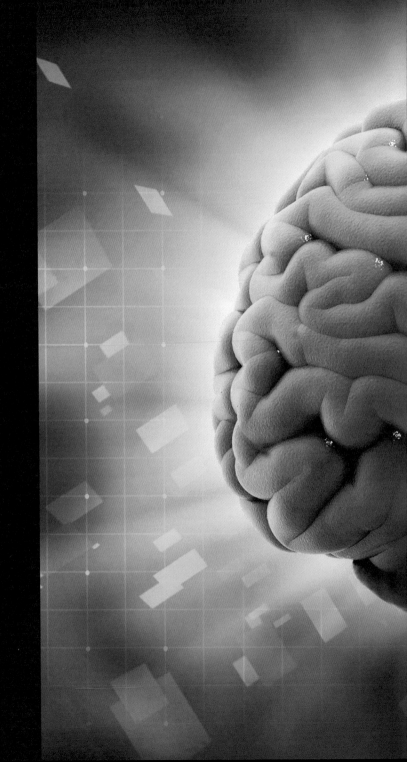

Our brain never gets tired. It works even if we are asleep. The brain does endless tasks. Our body temperature, blood pressure, heart rate and breathing are controlled by our powerful brain.

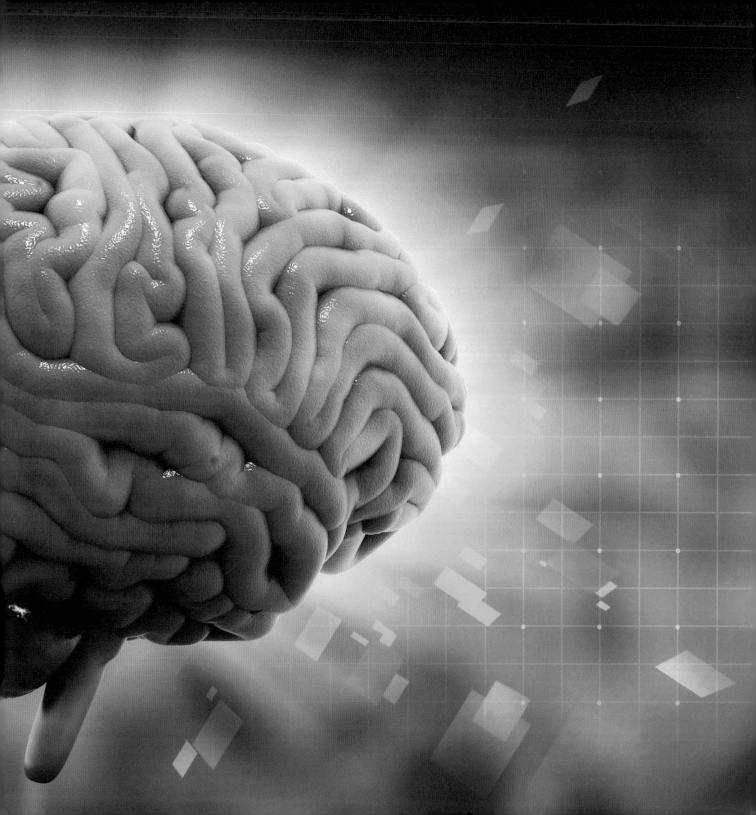

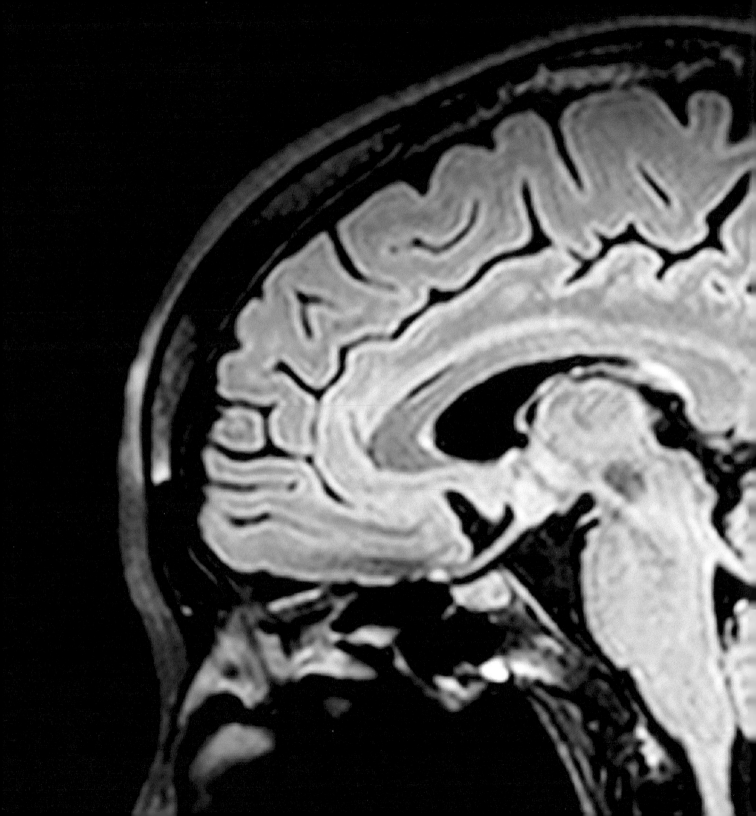

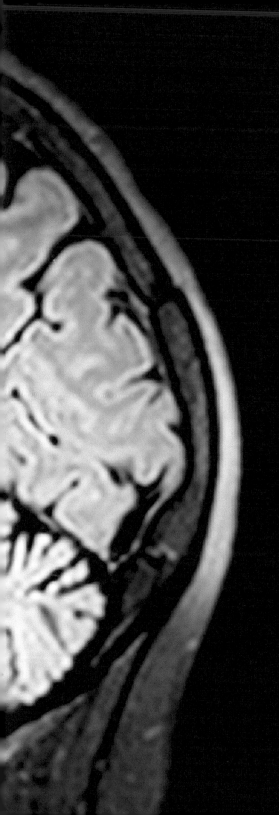

A flood of information comes into our bodies through our five sense, and our brain processes it. Our physical movements are handled by our active brain. All these are pretty cool!

Our brain is composed of billions of microscopic cells called neurons. Electrical and chemical messages are sent to our body by the neurons. The human brain is the control center of our nervous system.

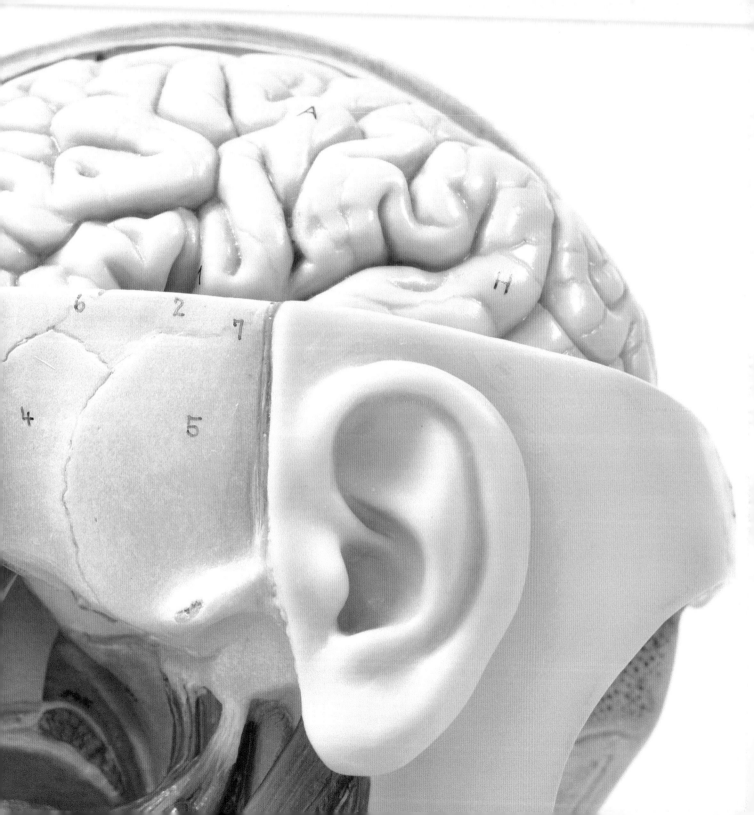

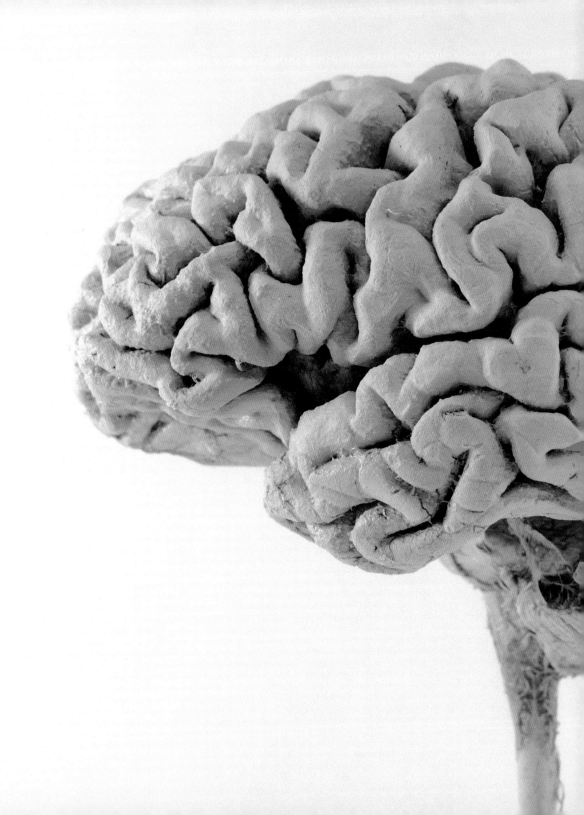

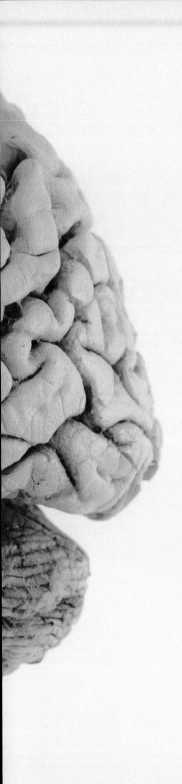

The neurons do a fantastic job of gathering and transmitting electrochemical signals. They are compared to the wires in a computer

Scientists still do not understand the human brain's complicated properties. Interestingly, the left side of the brain directs the right side of the body. Likewise, the right side of the brain manages the left side of the body.

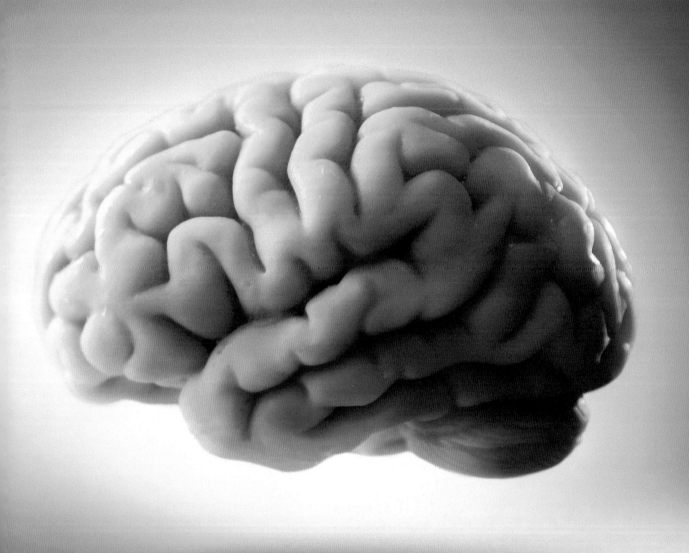

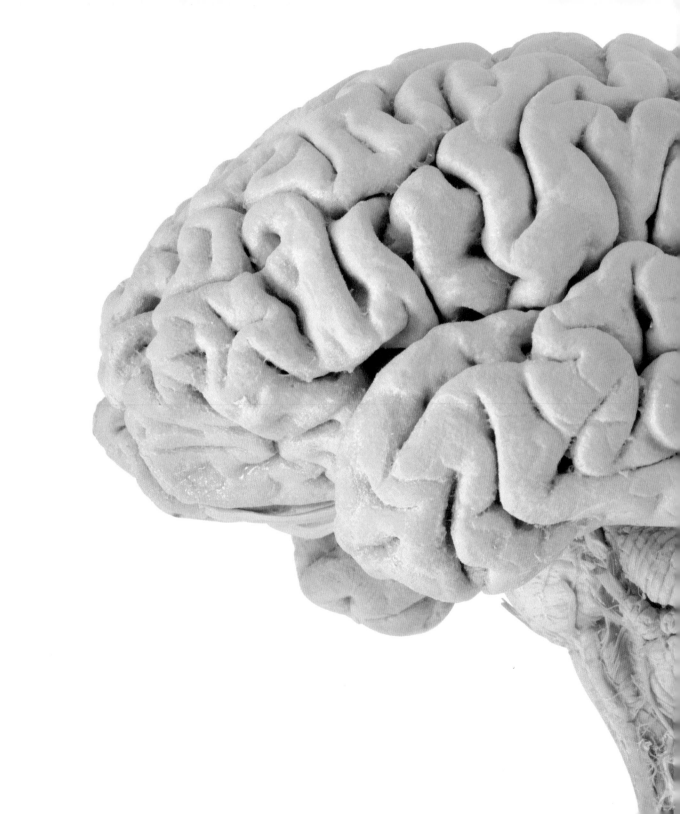

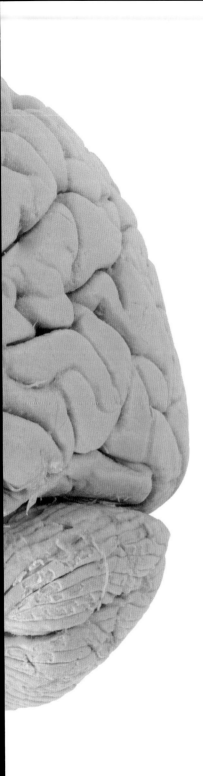

A lot of information comes into the brain through the spinal cord which connects to the base of the brain. But what we see and hear go directly into the brain. This is why people who are completely paralyzed can still see and hear.

The cerebrum
is the largest
part of the
human brain.

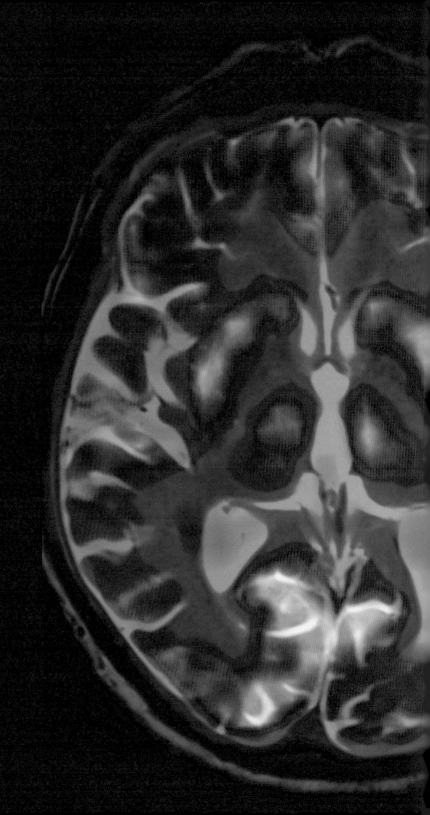

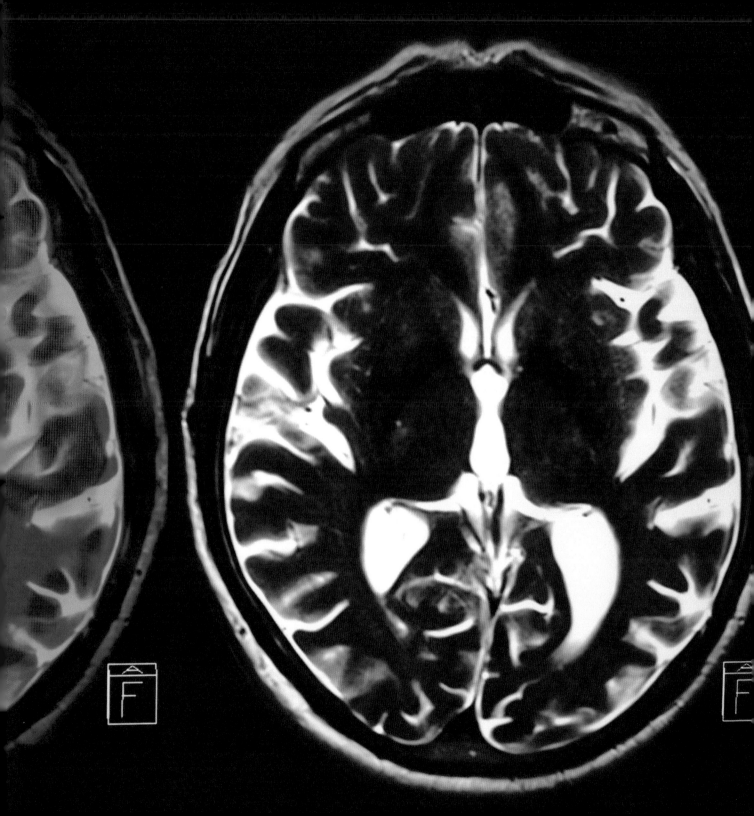

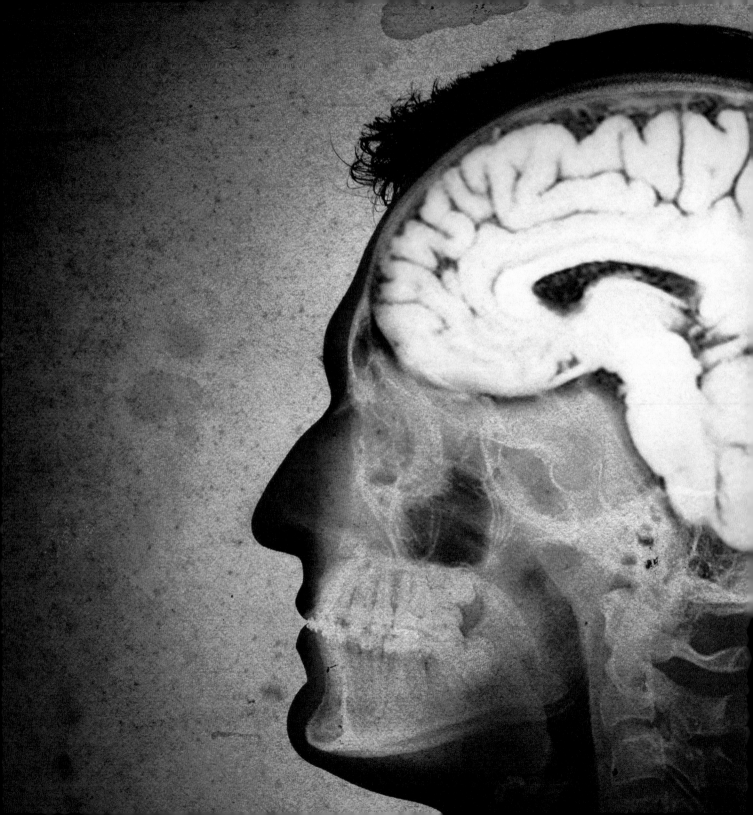

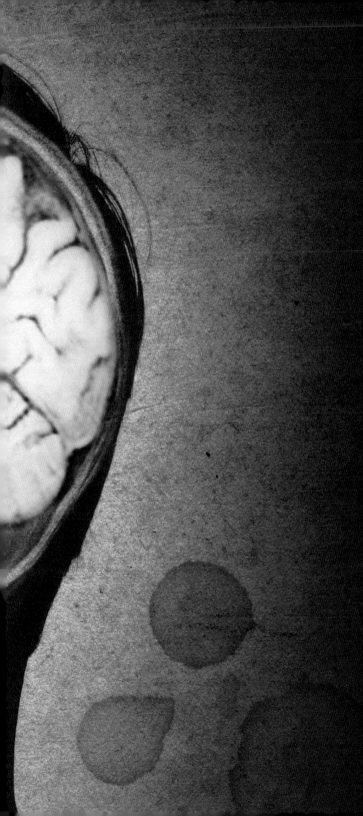

The other important parts of the human brain are the cerebral cortex, corpus callosum, thalamus, cerebellum, hypothalamus, hippocampus and the brain stem. Each part has a vital role in total brain function.

Our brain is protected by a casing made up of 22 bones that are joined together. This is called the cranium or the skull.

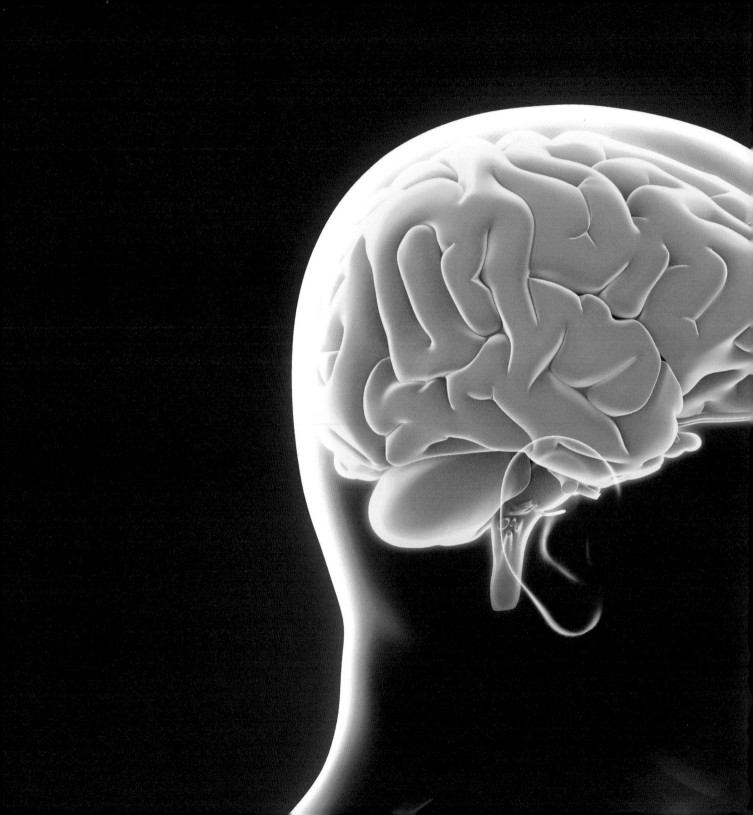

Surprisingly, the human brain is just 2% of the body's weight, around 3 pounds. Yes, it comprises little of our body weight— but our brain uses 20% of our body's energy.

Your brain is floating in a liquid known as cerebrospinal fluid. It helps protect your brain from impact and infections.

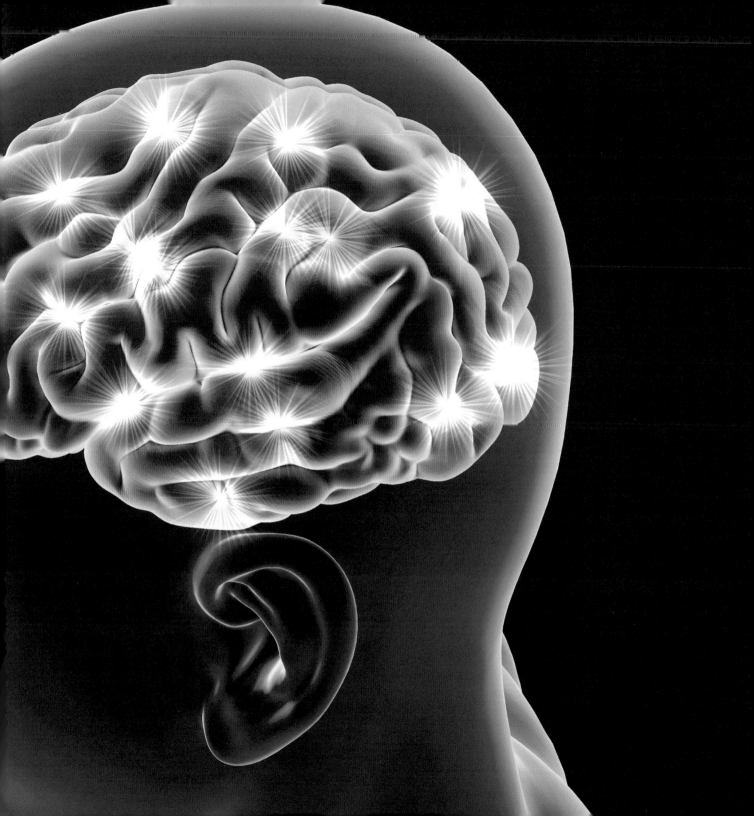

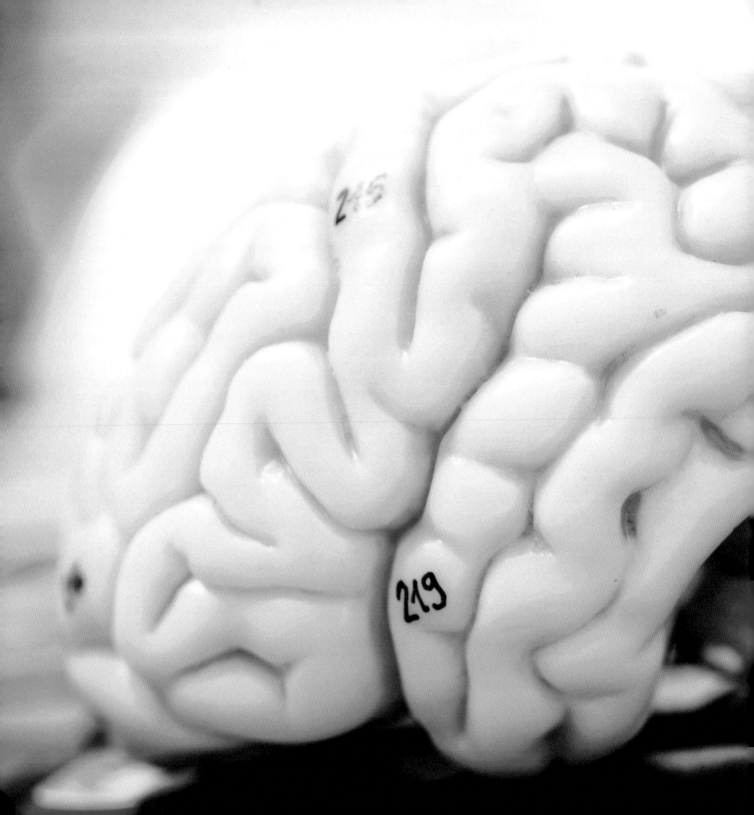

The neurons are connected by tiny pathways. That is why if you do things over and over again, like practicing a musical instrument, the pathways that the activity uses to send signals to the brain are strengthened.

If you seldom
do things, the
pathways get
weak. This
supports the
saying that
practice makes
perfect! If
you practice
doing things you
find difficult,
there comes a
timewhen the
things start to
get easier.

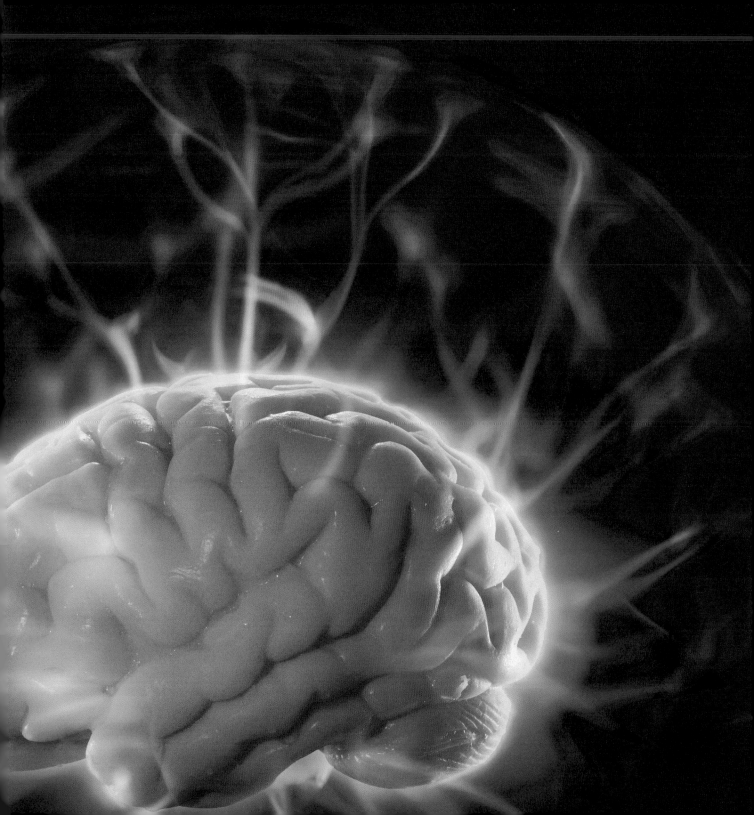

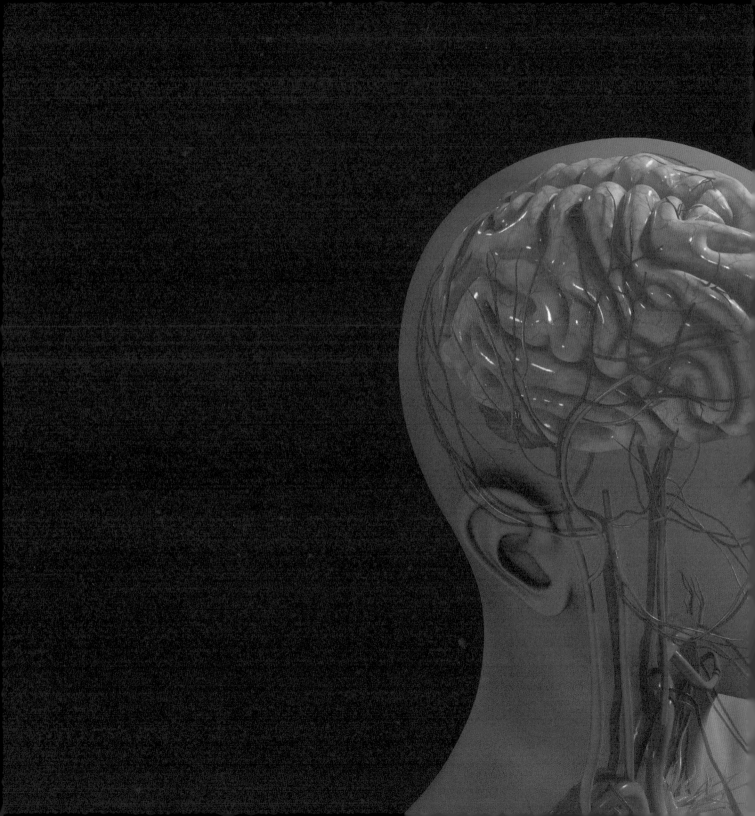

Kids, aren't you amazed about what your brain can do? Think about it! Whew, you're using your brain right now! You think, you dream, you reasonthings out, and you feel different emotions because of your big boss up there, right behind your eyes!

Printed in Great Britain
by Amazon